Daily Meditations
for
Women Who
Love Too Much

Other books by Robin Norwood

Women Who Love Too Much

Letters from Women Who Love Too Much

Why . . . A Guide to Answering Life's Toughest Questions

Other books illustrated by Richard Torregrossa

The Little Book of Wisdom

Daily Meditations
for
Women Who
Love Too Much

Robin Norwood

ILLUSTRATED BY
Richard Torregrossa

Jeremy P. Tarcher/Putnam
a member of Penguin Putnam Inc.
New York

Most Tarcher/Putnam books are available at special quantity discounts for bulk purchases for sales promotions, premiums, fund-raising, and educational needs. Special books or book excerpts also can be created to fit specific needs. For details, write or telephone Putnam Special Markets, 200 Madison Ave., New York, NY 10016; (212) 951-8891.

Jeremy P. Tarcher/Putnam
a member of Penguin Putnam Inc.
200 Madison Avenue
New York, NY 10016
http://www.putnam.com

Library of Congress Cataloging-in-Publication Data

Norwood, Robin.
Daily meditations for women who love too much /
Robin Norwood : illustrated by Richard Torregrossa
p.   cm.
ISBN 0-87477-876-X (alk. paper)
1. Relationship addiction.   2. Women—Mental health.
3. Women—Psychology.   4. Love.   5. Affirmations.   I. Title.
RC552.R44N65   1997   97-10244 CIP
616.858227—dc21

Book design by Judith Stagnitto Abbate
Cover design by Tanya Maiboroda
Cover illustration © 1997 by Richard Torregrossa

Printed in the United States of America
1   3   5   7   9   10   8   6   4   2

This book is printed on acid-free paper. ∞

Acknowledgments

First, I would like to thank Robin Norwood for giving me the opportunity to illustrate her wonderful insights. I would also like to thank Joel Fotinos, our editor, for his patient guidance and unique problem-solving abilities.

—RICHARD TORREGROSSA

To Barb A.,
who planted the seed

Introduction

The idea for this book first came during a conversation with a woman who had been greatly helped by reading and studying *Women Who Love Too Much*. She mentioned that a book of daily meditations would have been welcome during her struggle to recover from her lifelong pattern of addictive relationships.

You now hold the result of her suggestion in your hands—a first-aid manual to help you preserve your sanity, serenity, and sense of humor as you develop a healthier approach to living and loving. Richard Torregrossa's illustrations provide welcome leavening to a serious subject and at the same time place these daily reminders in a context as unexpectedly familiar as a surprise view of our own reflection.

For the most part the thoughts on each page

are brief and to the point, necessarily small doses of a new way of thinking to match the necessarily small steps we take, one by one, to change the direction of our lives.

ROBIN NORWOOD
Santa Barbara
March 1997

*A*sking a man to illustrate a book by a woman for women might at first seem like a peculiar choice. But what I found extraordinary about this work is that the issues addressed here, though written from a woman's perspective, transcend gender. The quest for love, the need for spirituality, and the eternal riddle of relationships all are topics of great concern to men as well as women. This book, then, is for all those who desire a greater understanding of themselves and the people they are trying to love.

RICHARD TORREGROSSA
San Diego
March 1997

When being in love means being in pain, we are loving too much.

$\mathcal{L}$oving turns into loving too much when your partner is inappropriate, uncaring, or unavailable, and yet you cannot give him up—in fact, you want him, you need him even more.

*T*here is such a thing as making one or two foolish choices in one's love life, but there is also such a thing as the very real disease of relationship addiction.

*W*henever we attempt to force a solution
to another's problem, we are loving too much.

$\mathscr{B}$eing women who love too much, we operate as though love, attention, and approval don't count unless we are able to extract them from men who, because of their own problems and preoccupations, are unable to readily give them to us.

*L*ike compulsive eaters, we who love too much must learn to do in a sane and balanced way what we once did obsessively. Because eating and relating both are necessary aspects of normal living, there is no clear-cut behavioral definition for sobriety.

Recovery is not, therefore, a black-and-white question but one of degree, relative to our former condition and behavior.

$\mathcal{W}$e begin by becoming *willing* to channel the energy and effort that we formerly spent on trying to change someone else toward changing ourselves instead.

*Y*ou need to recover from loving too much for your own sake; but when you stop suffering, your recovery may be so appealing that others watching may begin to pursue their own.

Recovery can be just as contagious as addiction and coaddiction are.

If we want to stop loving too much, first we change how we act, then how we think, and finally how we feel. If we wait until we feel differently before we behave differently, we will never change, never recover.

*N*one of us has invented a new variety of horrible secret or terrible loss. The secrets we keep keep us from recovering.

*I*t is an act of irresponsible self-indulgence to cite our childhood histories as *excuses* for any of our present behaviors, attitudes, or qualities that are less than healthy.

The difficult circumstances and unhappy effects of those childhood years provide *clues* to the very conditions we are meant, in this lifetime, to experience, overcome, understand, and forgive.

*P*ain is our wisest teacher knocking at our door.

*Y*ou cannot apply *self-help* to a problem from which the *self* that's trying to provide the *help* still suffers.

What is needed is spiritual help rather than self-help, an invocation of God's will rather than further indulgence in self-will.

$\mathcal{N}$o one can save us from the work our soul would have us do. Trouble comes when we try to avoid or postpone that work.

We may have learned as children that saying our prayers demonstrates our devotion to God—and if He is convinced of our sincerity, our requests of Him might be granted.

In spite of all our adult sophistication, when we think now about praying, we may do so with the same underlying attitude still in place.

But prayer isn't a way of placating God, staying in His good graces in order to get what we want. Our Higher Power doesn't need us to pray, isn't angry or disappointed if we don't. We are under no compunction to pray. The choice is entirely ours.

When we pray, we attune ourselves to a depth of love, wisdom, understanding, and guidance far greater than our personalities can generate.

When we pray, we avail ourselves of help from a Power that can do for us what we, on our own, cannot.

When we pray, if we align our wills with our Higher Power's will for us, our lives automatically become more manageable and we know greater freedom, greater serenity, and greater peace.

January 15

*N*o other area is as "slippery" as relation- ships are for clean and sober women. Most sober alcoholic women who slip do so over men.

We can love too much with children, too. When a parent overdoes caretaking of a child, that child is burdened by responsibility for the parent's welfare.

*S*ometimes we grieve when people leave or conditions change or things are removed that we would never willingly surrender, because we cannot yet see the greater good that is coming to us.

One of the more difficult tasks you face in your recovery is learning to say and do *nothing*. When his life is unmanageable, when everything in you wants to take over, to advise and encourage him, to manipulate the situation in whatever way you can, you must learn to hold still, to respect this other person enough to allow the struggle to be his, not yours. Your proper work lies in facing your own fears regarding what might happen to him and to your relationship if you let go of managing everything—and then going to work on eliminating your fears rather than manipulating him.

 $\mathcal{S}$ ome very addictive relationships are between same-sex lovers.

As women who love too much, we may actually relish our costarring roles in the recurring dramas and melodramas that make up our lives.

Believing that we have had the *saddest* childhood or the *most dangerous* lover or the *most shocking* experience can become our way of feeling important and getting attention from others. Recovery may feel dull by comparison.

When we stop loving too much, our relationship problems aren't automatically solved; but we do remove an enormous impediment to dealing with normal problems in healthy and productive ways.

*O*ur primary aim should be protecting our own serenity and well-being, rather than finding the right man. Then and only then are we able to begin to choose a companion who can care about us in a wholesome way, because the more we heal our own damage and the less we *need* from a partner, the more able we are to choose someone who isn't so damaged or needy himself.

$\mathcal{O}$ur needs can be met in many ways if we let go of our self-will and self-pity and the idea that we should be able to extract all our good from a given source, such as a man.

*O*ne of the primary features of loving too much is tremendous dependency, often masked by apparent strength.

When someone you love is in trouble, ask yourself, "Whose problem is it?"

Your problem is not that someone you love is in trouble, but your *feelings* when you are watching that person's struggle. Unless you can let go of having to fix it, you may need to stop watching.

When you begin to let go of controlling others in your life, you may actually feel physically as though you are falling off a cliff. The sensation of being out of control of yourself when you release others can be alarming. Here your spiritual practice can really help, because instead of letting go into a void, you can relinquish control of both yourself and those you love to a Higher Power.

*B*ecause relationship addicts need to be needed, we can actually sabotage growth in others by taking too much responsibility for bringing it about.

Remember: Another's journey is in God's hands, *just as yours is.*

*M*ost of the insanity and despair you experience comes directly from trying to manage and control what you cannot—him and his life. Think about all the attempts you've made: the endless speeches, the pleading, threats, bribes, maybe even violence. And remember, too, how you've felt after each failed attempt. Your self-esteem slipped another notch, and you became more anxious, more helpless, more filled with anger. The only way out of all this is to let go, because he will almost never change in the face of pressure from you. Even if you do finally get to hear him say you are the reason he's giving up a behavior, later on you'll find that you're also the reason he gives for resuming it.

$\mathcal{F}$or so many of us, the key to recovery is in learning to do the opposite of what we've always done.

$\mathcal{L}$earn to live without having your focus be on a man either as your problem or as the solution to your problem.

*T*he best preparation for your future is achieving greater understanding and acceptance of yourself and of all those who have already been in your life.

We make a great mistake when we put our order in to our Higher Power for a specific man, material thing, or result, since we can never know as well as that Higher Power does what truly is for our greatest good.

Our affirmations should always be invitations for spiritual expansion and guidance rather than self-willed demands for this or that specific thing, event, or person.

*W*hen you confront someone from whom you need a certain kind of response, you are not confronting at all—you are begging, perhaps with anger.

The more you need a specific reaction from an individual, the more dependent you are on that individual for your own well-being—and the more you are likely to encounter only his or her defenses.

*S*ay prayers for the willingness, the strength, and the courage to look honestly at your past—and at your part in it.

The psyche hears such efforts at house-cleaning and cooperates by bringing forth the buried pain of the past so that it can be consciously released.

As soon as our willingness to forgive the past is truly genuine, a great breakthrough of understanding comes and the pain of that past drops away.

$\mathcal{R}$ecovery from loving too much is very demanding spiritual work which requires that we surrender old and often dearly held anger and self-righteousness.

As our souls try to learn their lessons in order to draw closer to perfection, they choose the life conditions that will give them the opportunity to do so. This is why nowhere in spiritual teachings will you ever find it written that someone else is to blame for your present condition.

When you stop taking care of him and take care of yourself instead, the man in your life may become very angry and accuse you of not caring about him anymore. This anger generates from his panic at having to become responsible for his own life. As long as he can fight with you, make you promises, or try to win you back, his struggle is outside, with you, and not inside with himself. Give him back his life, and take back your own.

$\mathcal{S}$ometimes relationship addicts prefer fantasy relationships over involvement with real, live human beings.

Choosing unavailable persons on whom to focus is a great way of avoiding the tests of intimacy.

*A*nger and hatred toward another person tie us to that person with bonds of iron.

Unless we can forgive, we will return to that inappropriate relationship or become involved in others that are similar, and act out our drama over and over again.

But by forgiving and asking for forgiveness (or making amends), we release and are released.

*I*f your soul's lesson is to forgive, you must first experience the unforgivable. Otherwise, where is the lesson?

Bless and forgive and, at least in your heart, *ask forgiveness from* all the men (and the women, too) with whom you've ever fought and struggled in the past.

When we *forgive,* we *give* good *for* bad, and we are finished with the lesson.

When a woman who loves too much gives up her crusade to change the man in her life, he is then left to ponder the consequences of his own behavior. Since she is no longer frustrated and unhappy, but rather is becoming more and more excited about life, the contrast to his own troubled existence intensifies. No matter what he then chooses to do, by accepting the man in her life exactly as he is, a woman becomes free, one way or another, to live her own life—happily ever after.

$\mathcal{F}$orgiving doesn't mean allowing ourselves to be hurt again; it means, among other things, detaching so that we don't take another's actions toward us so personally.

Far from making us weak people who can be stepped on by others, forgiveness frees us so that we never have to allow ourselves to be treated badly again.

February 12

*A*ll diseases of addiction, including loving too much, imply both the violation of one's value system and the inability to stop or change through one's own efforts. Self-will must be surrendered and the help of a Higher Will invoked.

At our worst we women who love too much are relationship addicts, "man junkies" strung out on pain, fear, and yearning. As if this weren't bad enough, men may not be the only thing we're hooked on.

Not every woman who loves too much also eats too much or drinks too much or uses too many drugs, but for those of us who do, our recovery from relationship addiction must go hand in hand with our recovery from addiction to whatever substance we abuse.

A vicious cycle is created when physical dependence on a substance is exacerbated by the stress of an unhealthy relationship, and emotional dependence on a relationship is intensified by the chaotic feelings engendered by physical addiction.

We use being without a man or being with

the wrong man to explain and excuse our physical addiction. Conversely, our continued use of the addictive substance allows us to tolerate our unhealthy relationship by numbing our pain and robbing us of the motivation necessary for change.

We blame one for the other. We use one to deal with the other. And we become more and more hooked on both.

*Y*our soul has designed this life for you in order for you to learn its lessons. Be grateful for all those people who have been your teachers.

*M*any women make the mistake of looking for a man with whom to develop a relationship without first developing a relationship with themselves; they run from man to man, looking for what is missing within. The search must begin at home, within the self. No one can ever love us enough to fulfill us if we do not love ourselves, because when in our emptiness we go looking for love, we can find only more emptiness.

*I*f our addiction is our path to God, then we must be grateful for it.

*T*welve-step programs can provide the *primary* source of recovery from addictions, including relationship addiction, and counseling can serve as an adjunct, but not vice versa.

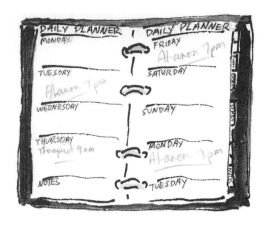

A rule of thumb is: The more difficult it is to end a relationship that is bad for you, the more elements of your personal childhood struggle it contains. When you are loving too much, very likely you are trying to overcome the old fears, anger, frustration, and pain from childhood—and to stop doing so seems tantamount to surrendering a precious opportunity for both obtaining what was always missing in your life and rectifying the many ways you have been wronged.

However, unless you change your patterns of relating, you're insuring that your adult years will be as full of pain as your childhood was— and adulthood lasts a lot longer. . . .

*T*he possibility of contracting AIDS through sexual encounters that are part of a desperate search for "Mr. Right" finally puts the life-threatening nature of relationship addiction in a clear light.

$\mathcal{A}$ need for control is often operating in women who team up with much younger men, just as in men who team up with much younger women.

*V*ery few models exist of people relating as peers in healthy, mature, honest, nonmanipulative, and nonexploitative ways, probably for two reasons: First, in all honesty, such relationships in real life are fairly rare. Second, since the quality of emotional interplay in a healthy relationship is often much subtler than the blatant conflict of an unhealthy relationship, its dramatic potential is usually overlooked in literature, drama, and songs. If unhealthy styles of relating plague us, perhaps it is partly because that is very nearly all we see and all we know.

*N*o relationship can save you from the pain of your history. Until you walk through your pain, you'll simply repeat your history.

$\mathscr{I}$t is both naive and presumptuous to tell a man what he should do in order to be with you. He is who he is. Are you willing to accept that?

*T*he sex act, when it is highly gratifying physically, has the power to create deeply felt bonds between two people. For women who love too much, especially, the intensity of our struggle with a man may contribute to the intensity of our sexual experience with him and thus our bond to him. And the converse is also true. When we are involved with a man who is not so much of a challenge, the sexual dimension may also lack fire and passion. Because we are not in an almost constant state of excitement over him, and because sex isn't used to prove something, we may find an easier, more relaxed relationship to be somewhat tame. Compared to the tempestuous styles of relating that we've known, this tamer kind of experience only seems to verify for us that tensions, struggle, heartache, and drama truly do equal "real" love.

*I*t is a spiritual principle that we will continue to encounter others who will embody the opportunity for us to learn our most pressing lesson. When we learn to overcome the problem *in ourselves,* our "teachers" will fade away.

When we stop *our* half of the battle, the battle is over.

*B*oredom is the sensation that we women who love too much so often experience when we find ourselves with "nice" men: no bells peal, no rockets explode, no stars fall from heaven. In the absence of excitement we feel antsy, irritable, and awkward, a generally uncomfortable state that is covered by the label *boredom*. Our skills at relating are honed for challenge, not for simply enjoying a man's company. There is more discomfort in the presence of steady, dependable, cheerful, stable fellows than there ever is with men who are unresponsive, emotionally distant, unavailable, or uninterested.

WW♥2M
3 miles

*R*emember, most addicts, whatever their addiction, do not recover. Most eventually die of their addiction.

Try to take your relationship addiction as seriously as you would cancer. Become willing to go to any lengths to recover.

When we accept what we cannot change, and change what we can, we create for ourselves a climate of healing.

$\mathcal{T}$o stop loving too much, you must lay aside your fantasy of being the one who will make all the difference in this man's life. That's *your* need, and it's not a healthy one.

*S*ex is one of the tools we who love too much use for manipulating or changing our partners. We behave seductively to get our own way, and we feel great when it works and bad when it doesn't. Failing to get what we want usually causes us to try even harder.

We often find it very exciting to be involved in the power struggles inherent in our attempts to manipulate the men in our lives. We confuse anxiety, fear, and pain with love and sexual excitement. We call the sensation of having a knot in the stomach "love."

$\mathcal{N}$ever make threats you're not prepared to carry out. In fact, never make threats at all.

$\mathcal{M}$any of us have been taught that good sex means real love, and that, conversely, sex couldn't be really satisfying and fulfilling if the relationship as a whole were not right for us. Nothing could be farther from the truth for women who love too much. Because of the dynamics operating at every level of our interactions with men, including the sexual level, a difficult or impossible relationship may actually contribute to sex being exciting, passionate, and compelling.

*W*hen we feel responsible for another's behavior and we cannot bear our guilt and anguish, we need help *in managing our own uncomfortable feelings,* not help in managing that other person's life.

March 6

We may be hard pressed to explain to family and friends how someone who is not particularly admirable or even very likable can nevertheless arouse in us a thrill of anticipation and an intensity of longing never matched by what we feel for someone kinder or more presentable. It is difficult to articulate that we are enchanted by the dream of calling forth all the positive attributes—the love, caring, devotion, integrity, and nobility—we are sure are lying dormant in our lover, waiting to blossom in the warmth of our love.

How can we explain that it isn't the person he *is* that we find so attractive, but the person we're convinced we can help him *become?* How can we admit to ourselves or others that we're in love with someone who doesn't yet exist, and enchanted with our power to make him appear?

*T*he best rule of thumb for dealing with people whose lives are unmanageable is to scrupulously avoid doing *anything* for them that they could do for themselves *if they chose.*

March 8

Women who love too much often tell themselves the man with whom they are involved has never really been loved before, not by his parents, nor by his previous wives or girlfriends. We see him as damaged and readily take on the task of making up for all that was missing in his life long before we ever met him. We take his emotional unavailability, his anger or depression or cruelty or indifference or violence or dishonesty or addiction, for signs that he has not been loved enough. We pit our love against his faults, his failings, even his pathology. We are determined to save him through the power of our love.

*I*t is never too late to heal ourselves and our relationships, even with people who are no longer alive. People's souls endure, just as ours do, and respond to our changes of heart.

*A*ll each of us really knows about parenting is what we experienced as children with our own parents . . . and what some of us learned from them was more about what *not* to do than about how to parent well.

We need to appreciate *everything*, positive and negative, we've received from our parents because *all* of it has in some way contributed to our own conscious efforts at this difficult business of loving.

What is most hidden in us is also what is most universal. *Everyone* has secrets that need to be uncovered and healed, and as we face our own, we help create a climate in which others can do the same. As we work on our own healing, we help bring about healing in the world.

*I*nformation alone, no matter how alarming, is simply not enough to stop any kind of addiction.

*D*iseases of addiction, unlike other diseases, lay siege to *every* dimension of the person afflicted: the emotional and spiritual as well as the physical. With the relationship–addicted woman, it isn't just her love relationship that is affected. Her interactions with friends, family members, coworkers, and children all suffer from her obsession with a man. Her health is damaged from prolonged stress, and her contact with her own spiritual side is diminished.

*T*ry too hard to help a man and you'll find yourself playing "controlling mother" to his "naughty child."

$\mathcal{V}$ery few of us who love too much have a conviction, at the core of our being, that we deserved to love and be loved simply because we exist. We believe instead that we harbor terrible faults or flaws and that we must do good works in order to make up for this. We live with guilt that we have these shortcomings and in terror of being found out. We work very, very hard at trying to appear to be good because we don't believe we are.

*I*n relationship addiction, an underlying fear of closeness coexists with an even greater fear of abandonment.

*M*any women who love too much also eat too much or spend too much. Addictions aren't discrete entities; they overlap in their physical and emotional roots. In fact, recovery from one addiction may actually cause another addiction to accelerate.

Fortunately, the same steps for recovery apply equally well to all addictions.

$\mathcal{W}$omen who come from violent homes tend to choose violent partners; women who grew up with alcoholism tend to choose chemically dependent partners; and so on. One dynamic always present in relationship addiction is the unconscious drive to re-create the struggle from the past, and this time, to *win*.

A will of iron operating in interpersonal relationships can be concealed by alternately assuming the roles of helper and victim.

$\mathcal{U}$ntil we understand to the core of our being that one man or another will never be the answer to our difficulties, we are prisoners of our own patterns of addictive relating.

*E*very woman who loves too much can stop her obsessive behavior for a while, but permanent control through self-will is a deadly illusion: true recovery comes only after surrender.

March 22

*T*here are no accidents regarding those to whom we have compulsory attachments—our fathers, our mothers, and all the rest.

The difficulties our parents and other family members may embody for us are gifts from our souls to our personalities. Through the friction generated in these inescapable relationships, many of our deepest character defects are eventually worn away.

$\mathcal{W}$e must give up the role that has served us long and in some ways well—the role of victim, martyr, rescuer, or self-righteous avenger—or perhaps all of these in turn.

There is an old joke about a nearsighted man who has lost his keys late at night and is looking for them by the light of a streetlamp. Another person comes along and offers to help him look, but asks him, "Are you sure this is where you lost them?" He answers, "No, but this is where the light is."

Are you, like the man in the story, searching for what is missing in your life not where there is some hope of finding it, but where, because you are a woman who loves too much, it is easiest to look?

*N*o man will ever be the "right" one until we heal that in ourselves which has been attracted to a battle of wills, has needed to win or to lose, and then has pointed the finger of blame at another for our troubles.

March 26

*W*hat an irony it is that some of us want to travel backward and forward in time and from one end of the globe to the other, searching for enlightenment, when our soul's work is always right in front of us.

*N*othing is meant to stay the same. If we don't progress, we decline.

*W*hen an emotionally painful event occurs and we tell ourselves it is our fault, we are actually saying that we have control of it: If we change, the pain will stop. This dynamic is behind much of the self-blame in women who love too much. By blaming ourselves, we hold on to the hope that we will be able to figure out what we are doing wrong and then correct it, thereby controlling the situation and stopping the pain.

Our task is to face the situation, accept that it is painful, let go of our *illusion* of control, and ask for support and guidance from a Higher Will.

$\mathcal{W}$e do not enter into significant relationships by accident. We are inexorably drawn to
the partners with whom we have the opportunity to learn our most pressing personal and
interpersonal lessons. Acknowledging that we
are not victims of, but rather volunteers for, the
challenges with which love presents us can accelerate our learning those lessons.

As we move toward recovery from loving too much, *no* step we take is really small, because each one changes the direction of our lives.

We need to remember that life on this Earth is a classroom, and that as one advances through school, the tasks become more complicated.

Every grade in this school of life is necessary to our ultimate development. Each is challenging when we are at that level, but as soon as we have mastered one level, we must go on to the next. None of us, having learned what second grade has to teach us, would want to stay there forever. Instead, we eagerly embrace our next course of study.

So if your life seems very difficult, try to keep in mind that your present challenges indicate not only what is still to be learned, but also how far you've come, how much you've already mastered. Learning not to love too much is a very different kind of lesson than, for example, learning not to steal.

Learn not to overdo compassion. Surrender both your self-will and the people you love to a Higher Will. These challenges are as subtle as they are profound.

April 1

$\mathscr{B}$ecause Nature seems to abhor a vacuum as much in the areas of human behavior and emotions as in physics, we cannot simply stop loving too much without substituting another (hopefully more positive) behavior to take its place.

The more lovingly and generously we treat ourselves, the less likely we are to allow anyone else to treat us badly.

April 3

*I*f you want, too badly, to save people you love from the suffering attendant to their addictive behavior, think about this question:

Who could have saved me?

There were probably lots of people who tried: girlfriends, your mother, a sister or brother, maybe even your children . . . and quite possibly all their sincere efforts only caused you to dig in deeper.

Learn to honor the transformative process as it unfolds in those you love—and not to interfere.

We have the power to give ourselves love and caring: it isn't necessary to wait, empty, until a man comes along to supply these.

*T*rying to recover from relationship addiction (or any other addiction) without faith is like walking up a steep hill backward in high heels.

*S*ometimes people need to be apart. But if you separate without learning the lesson that the relationship is trying to teach you, then you'll have to face it again in the next relationship, and again in the one after that.

When you can accept this man exactly as he is, without anger or resentment, without wanting to change him or punish him, without taking what he does or doesn't do personally, you will have deepened your soul and received the gift this relationship has been trying to give you.

After you've learned the lesson the relationship has been trying to impart, you may find that whether you stay or leave hasn't been the real issue at all.

*W*hen we pursue a man who cannot love us, we need to recognize there is a predatory element in the sexual chase, a desire to subjugate another person through one's own desirability.

A working definition of addiction can be: In spite of ample evidence that something isn't good for us, we cannot stop our involvement with it.

*W*hen we have been traumatized in any way, there is always the (usually unconscious) drive to re-create the traumatic situation and this time to prevail, to gain ascendancy over what has defeated us before.

The greater the trauma we have suffered, the more powerful the drive in us to re-create it and this time surmount it. This is one path to compulsion.

April 10

What we have known in our family of origin will always be most comfortable to us, *no matter how unhealthy that family of origin was.* It naturally follows that we choose in adult relationships that with which we are already familiar. After all, the word "familiar" is derived from the concept of family.

$\mathcal{I}$n recovery we no longer call a man up to tell him we aren't speaking to him anymore.

*I*f you truly want to recover from loving too much, you must take responsibility for the fact that you *chose* this partner and realize that there are lessons for you to learn in this relationship. The first lesson is how to let go of the determination to change another person.

The driving, compelling need to do *something*—to affect some change in another person—is one of the more destructive elements in relationship addiction.

Can you honestly say that every attempt to pressure your partner to change has been loving rather than coercive and manipulative?

*O*ur own recovery must always be our first priority if we want to be of help. In order to give something, we have to have it ourselves.

*I*f our interactions with men have been dangerous and dramatic and we start to recover, start to detach, our partners may try very hard to get us hooked back into the battle. And the part of us that still wants to win may want to go back and give it one more try, making all the familiar moves we know so well. But we who are relationship addicts must question very closely our motives for reengaging with dangerous people who have been our "drug."

$\mathcal{R}$emember, it is anger and fear rather than love that keep most people struggling in unhealthy ways with each other.

Since people can divorce each other and still continue these struggles for years, the issue is obviously not as simple as whether to stay or to leave.

When we feel we have the answer for other people, that they are wrong and we are right, we are being *self-righteous,* a state that cannot coexist with the humility and surrender necessary for our recovery.

Being self-righteous, believing that we know exactly what the truth is regarding right and wrong, can unfortunately serve as one of the more impenetrable defenses against waking up to our own condition.

April 17

*C*hanging requires not a prodigious, dramatic, temporary assault on the problem, but a daily surrender and commitment.

*I*t isn't what we tell our daughters, but rather how we feel and act, that provides their most formative lessons in what it is to be a woman. Although our own recovery from relationship addiction doesn't guarantee our daughters won't repeat our pattern, it's still the best insurance against their doing so. In fact, a relationship-addicted mother's greatest gift to her daughter is her own ongoing recovery.

Isn't it comforting to know that the better care we take of ourselves, the more we create the opportunity for true health and happiness in all the people around us?

What we must do to protect our own recovery doesn't always appear to others as the "nice" thing. However, living with diseases of addiction and coaddiction requires that the rules of etiquette be suspended and the guidelines for recovery be followed instead.

Certain kinds of addictions lead people to make career choices that are reflections of their disease, because addicts often try to use their careers as a defense against their addiction. Hiding behind the role of "expert" can be a way of defending oneself against deep pain and dark secrets. How can one possibly have a problem in the area where one is the expert?

Relationship addicts most typically are drawn to careers in the helping professions. Many of us who choose the professions that involve helping others do so because we are damaged ourselves. We then use our work as a way of focusing on other people's lives and problems in order to avoid facing our own.

We have the most to offer others when we have our own recovery in hand.

$\mathcal{A}$s you learn to withdraw your obsessive attention from another's behavior, you are left without distraction from your own problems, which may be massive. This is difficult and frightening, but you will not recover from relationship addiction until you find the courage to focus on your own life rather than a man's.

$\mathcal{F}$or many of us, being with an addicted partner is easier than facing our own disease and
embarking on our own recovery.

Should our partners begin to recover, we must
either do so as well or find another man with
a problem.

Addiction of any kind creates the pressure that makes personal transformation possible, because recovery from addiction requires the surrender of the personal will to a Higher Will.

No one can surrender someone else's will, and therefore no one can bring about anyone else's recovery. Indeed, those of us who would try undoubtedly need to do some surrendering of our own.

*A*fter a lifetime of unhealthy relating, the woman who loves too much will often feel worse in the first stages of recovery, even as she begins to get better. This is because she goes into withdrawal from her old patterns of thinking and behaving, *all* of which must change in order for her to get well.

$\mathcal{E}$very recovery is a miracle that happens by grace but not by accident.

*T*o heal we need to face not only the buried memories from childhood but the extent of our own inappropriate choices and behaviors as adults.

*I*t is common for women who love too much to remain deliberately vague regarding the behaviors and inclinations of their partners. Such vagueness is dangerous.

*W*omen who are dedicated feminists and yet "man junkies" may find the roots of both their politics and their disease in the same childhood experiences: exposure and subjection to an angry, aggressive, dominant father and a resentful, docile, martyred mother.

*A*ddiction of any kind, whether to another person, a substance, or a behavior, is not immoral but simply amoral, like any other disease.

*R*elating compulsively loses its mystery when viewed as a driving but unconscious need to control in the present what was uncontrollable in our past. The more overwhelming the childhood experience(s), the greater the unconscious need—and compulsion—to re-create the same emotionally charged climate or situation in adulthood and attempt to master it.

A far healthier and more sane approach is to work on becoming *willing* to face whatever there is in our past that needs to be addressed and healed. When we are willing to face our past, our memories will begin unfolding as quickly as we are able to handle them.

Trust this.

As our buried history becomes part of our conscious awareness, our actions that relate to it become more conscious, too. Where once there was a compulsion, now we have a choice. It may not be an *easy* choice, because giving up old behavior patterns is uncomfortable. But when choice is possible, to deliberately repeat unhealthy behavior becomes even more uncomfortable than giving it up.

*N*o matter what kind of parents, what kind of childhood, what kind of traumas we have known, we can change our own inheritance from one of disease to one of recovery, if we make the choice to forgive and to heal.

*M*any women who love too much suspect they were incest victims. If you suspect you were, it's very likely to be true.

$\mathcal{C}$ompulsive eating is commonly present in women who have been sexually abused.

*W*e are *blessed* when life makes it impossible for us to go on as before, when we must change our behavior. But, of course, it doesn't feel like a blessing at the time.

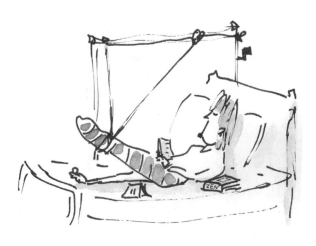

$\mathcal{T}$here is a natural human tendency toward denial. We often require various degrees of catastrophe to break through it.

$\mathcal{W}$e may have one addiction that covers up another, such as when an addiction to exercise helps disguise the effects of a compulsion to eat.

Relationship addiction, like drug abuse or alcoholism, is a progressive disease. That is, the time period between launching an addictive relationship and finding life completely unmanageable speeds up dramatically as the years go by.

*A*greeing to have contact with a man who has been our "drug" may have the same effect that taking a drink would have on a sober alcoholic. Years of recovery may be wiped out, and the obsession off and running stronger than ever.

$\mathcal{S}$ome men are like broccoli: not too exciting but wholesome and good for us; and some
men are like chocolate cake: incredibly appealing but, for those of us who are addictive,
definitely very dangerous.

If we are relationship addicts, we need to
learn to relate sanely and avoid those people
who are for us the drug that propels us head-
long into our disease.

*O*ur attempts to matter to this man, to become as necessary to his well-being as he is to ours, can turn us into clinging, smothering, manipulative, and even self-abasing women.

When we love too much, we are usually despised for all our efforts: our partner despises us, and we despise ourselves.

$\mathscr{N}$ot practicing an addiction requires more than just telling yourself to change.

*N*othing works better than prayer as long as we're asking for God's will and not our own.

$\mathcal{D}$o you begin a relationship by assuming the role of the all-giving, all-accepting, all-nurturing parent to his naughty, needy child?

We who love too much offer an unspoken deal to the men who strike us as needy: I'll take care of you first, and then you'll take care of me.

When we turn to a drug, a behavior, or another person to take care of an uncomfortable feeling, we run the risk of developing an unhealthy dependency.

If a man has come to represent relief from feelings of anxiety and abandonment, we can become desperately dependent on him. He is our "fix."

Our "fix" always costs us something in return for the temporary relief it brings. With relationship addiction, the cost is usually, at the very least, an emotional hangover.

$\mathcal{S}$obriety in relationships, while very real, is also very subtle and cannot be measured except by the eventual degree of serenity we achieve in our lives.

May 18

*I*f someone shocks or hurts you once, he will most likely do it again, except that you will have less right to be shocked or hurt because now you already know he has the capacity for that kind of behavior.

Since he's an adult, we'll assume he acted as he did, not because he didn't know better, but because that behavior is part of who he is. A man can put the brakes on for a while or let you put the brakes on for him for a while, but it's only temporary. Sooner or later he'll have to go back to being who he really is. If you don't let him, if you try to manage your partner's behavior or addiction, all your efforts will not ultimately generate feelings of gratitude in him. What he will feel toward you instead is resentment for getting between him and what he wants or needs to do. Then his behavior is no longer the problem. *You* are.

$\mathcal{I}$t is a lack of respect for another's right to be who he is that allows us to try to help him manage his life, *even when he appears to invite us to do so.*

When a man invites you to help him control any aspect of his life, he is setting a trap for you. *His* problem has just become *your* problem.

When a parent makes a companion and confidante of a child, a violation of that child's boundaries has occurred. Any child who is elevated to peer status by an adult has been taken over to serve the adult's need. In order to do no further harm and to obtain the solace, guidance, and support we need, we must turn to adult peers who are also seeking recovery from relationship addiction and will share with us their experience, strength, and hope.

May 21

*W*hen people are really trying to change, they don't talk about it much. They're too busy doing it.

*F*or most of us who are relationship addicts, it is so much easier to say, "This person is my problem," than to admit the fear and awkwardness of being consistently and intimately present with another.

*A*ll healing, whether of a broken leg or a broken mind or a broken heart, comes about through the operation of a spiritual principle.

This guiding spiritual principle exists in every one of us; contacting that principle is the quest born of every addiction, including loving too much.

Finding this spiritual principle within and surrendering to its guidance is *very* hard work, but if we are loving too much, not surrendering is much harder.

$\mathcal{E}$motional pain exists because we are not honestly acknowledging something about ourselves or our condition—something that, at some level, we *already know.*

*T*rue change demands a surrender that is tantamount to a crucifixion.

*A*s relationship addicts, we do just as much damage to our children as a practicing alcoholic would because . . .

- our mood swings are as erratic, dramatic, and unpredictable;

- our actions are just as driven, just as irrational when we need a "fix";

- our thoughts and feelings are nearly always focused elsewhere;

- we are as dangerous behind the wheel when we are under the influence of our out-of-control emotions;

- we become increasingly dishonest, putting the blame for our problems everywhere but on our own addiction.

*E*motional pain is to the psyche what physical pain is to the body: a signal that something is sick or damaged.

$\mathcal{L}$ife is, after all, about waking up and growing up. We make those processes more painful because we don't welcome them.

$\mathscr{I}$t is through seeking our recovery that our fearful secrets are transformed into our cherished gifts.

$\mathcal{I}$n recovery you will lose nothing that is truly for your own highest good.

May 31

*T*wo of recovery's promises are that life gets *better* and that we become *truly* helpful.

$\mathcal{E}$verything we do naturally in response to another's addiction is wrong.

Wanting to help and wanting to punish are codependent reactions.

$\mathcal{N}$ever, ever do more than half the work on another person's problem.

When we try too hard to help another, we feel frustration and anger, and that other person feels guilt and resentment.

Making necessary changes must be *more* important to the person who needs to do so than it is to those of us who would be of help.

*N*o therapist can be the paid solution to the client's problem.

Taking your life to a therapist is *not* like taking your car to a mechanic. *You* are still responsible for identifying and correcting whatever isn't working.

*P*eople rarely change except through unbearable pain: When we relieve another's pain, we often short-circuit that person's motivation to change. This is why most of our efforts to solve another's problems actually prolong and perpetuate those problems.

Unfortunately, when we love too much, another's tolerance for pain is usually greater than our tolerance for watching it. Instead of trying to fix the problems, we need to get out of the way of their consequences.

We are certain that if we show someone how much we love him, no matter how he treats us, he will change. What we are really showing him is that it is safe for him to remain the same.

*M*any women who love too much have serious problems with endogenous depression.

Trying to live a normal life while suffering from endogenous depression is a lot like trying to ski on a broken leg—very difficult and very painful.

When struggling with depression, *do not* aim for perfection. Rest and reduce your stress.

*R*ecovery means choosing only that which supports your serenity and well-being.

*A*lcohol puts to sleep the part of your brain that says "no"—and you know how important that part of your brain is when you're trying not to practice your particular style of loving too much.

Sometimes we want to call him or stop by his house or spend the night with him, even though we know that doing so is a big mistake.

So we drink first. Later, by telling ourselves we wouldn't have behaved as we did if we hadn't been drinking, we avoid taking responsibility for our choices and exploring their meaning in our life. And so our unhealthy cycle continues.

*L*oving yourself enough to become free of addiction is a prerequisite to loving another person.

*N*ever suppose that relationship addiction won't kill you. It is a condition that produces incredible stress, and we all know stress kills.

Become willing to go to whatever lengths are necessary in order to achieve your recovery. You are saving your life.

$\mathcal{R}$ecovery is an ongoing process that begins minute by minute, grows hour by hour,
and finally continues year after year, but it never
proceeds more than one day at a time.

$\mathcal{G}$o to any lengths not to do any of the little or big things that constitute a "slip," not to make any of the helpful or controlling or punishing moves that come so easily and insidiously to mind.

The belief that finding the right therapist would solve all of life's problems is nearly as widespread as the belief that finding the right man would do so. Recovery from any addiction, including loving too much, requires reliance not on a therapist but on a Higher Power.

*M*any of us, after our first recovery, discover we have a *next* recovery as well.

Recovery in one area often makes it clear how unmanageable life is in another area.

*I*t is the nature of women who love too much to greatly minimize how bad the situation has become. The attempts to control the obsession repeatedly fail, and there is an increasing disparity between one's public image and one's secret, private behavior.

*I*f relationship addiction is present, no other approach is likely to work as well as a twelve-step approach to recovery.

$\mathcal{B}$eing willing to learn a new way of living one day at a time is far more productive in the long run than trying too hard to go too fast.

The First Promise of Recovery from Relationship Addiction

We accept ourselves fully, even while wanting to change parts of ourselves. There is a basic self-love and self-regard, which we carefully nurture and purposely expand.

June 19

The Second Promise of Recovery from Relationship Addiction

We accept others as they are, without trying to change them to meet our needs.

*The Third Promise of Recovery
from Relationship Addiction*

*W*e are in touch with our feelings and attitudes about every aspect of our lives, including our sexuality.

The Fourth Promise of Recovery from Relationship Addiction

We cherish every aspect of ourselves: our personalities, our appearance, our beliefs and values, our bodies, our interests, and our accomplishments. We validate ourselves rather than searching for relationships to give us a sense of self-worth.

The Fifth Promise of Recovery from Relationship Addiction

*O*ur self-esteem is great enough that we can enjoy being with others, especially men, who are fine just as they are. We do not need to be needed in order to feel worthy.

June 23

The Sixth Promise of Recovery from Relationship Addiction

We allow ourselves to be open and trust-ing with appropriate people. We are not afraid to be known at a deeply personal level, but also we do not expose ourselves to the exploitation of those who are not interested in our well-being.

The Seventh Promise of Recovery from Relationship Addiction

We learn to question, "Is this relationship good for me? Does it enable me to grow into all I am capable of being?"

The Eighth Promise of Recovery from Relationship Addiction

When a relationship is destructive, we are able to let go of it without experiencing disabling depression. We have a circle of supportive friends and healthy interests to see us through crises.

The Ninth Promise of Recovery from Relationship Addiction

We value our own serenity above all else. All the struggles, drama, and chaos of the past have lost their appeal. We are protective of ourselves, our health, and our well-being.

The Tenth Promise of Recovery from Relationship Addiction

We know that a relationship, in order to work, must be between partners who share similar values, interests, and goals, and who each have a capacity for intimacy. We also know that we are worthy of the best that life has to offer.

The first phase of recovery from loving too much begins when we realize what we are doing and wish we could stop.

$\mathcal{A}$s we stop loving too much, we no longer base what we say and do on how we think the other person will react.

*A*s we recover, what once felt normal and familiar begins to feel uncomfortable and unhealthy.

$\mathcal{A}$s we stop loving too much, we no longer base what we say and do on how we think the other person will react.

*A*s we recover, what once felt normal and familiar begins to feel uncomfortable and unhealthy.

*R*esentments are like a Frankenstein's monster in that they take on a life of their own unless we work to free ourselves from them.

If you're not careful, you'll find you have a pet resentment that requires daily care and feeding.

$\mathcal{I}$f we tell the story of our victimization enough times to ourselves, eventually we'll have to tell it to nearly everyone else as well.

We do not receive more in life by wishing others less.

July 4

*N*othing in a relationship happens by accident or in a vacuum. That man is exactly who he was when you met him and decided to be with him. We who love too much may be intrigued by and attracted to the very qualities we also decide to try to change in a man.

Refuse to regard yourself as a victim in a relationship. Acknowledge that you have fully participated in whatever games have gone on.

July 6

*W*ith any difficult partner, become willing
to look at what *your* steps are in the dance.

*A*dmitting that there are no accidents in relationships and that we are not victims forces us to grow up and face our own dark side.

$\mathcal{T}$rue recovery occurs when we give up seeing the problem as outside ourselves and within someone else.

*T*o overcome resentment, bless the other person and pray for his highest good.

When we are envious, we are caught in the mistaken belief that there isn't enough good in the world for everybody.

$\mathcal{W}$e receive what we send out—so send out blessings!

We of each sex would do well to understand ourselves better. We probably cannot ever hope to be experts on each other.

*A*ny behavior between human beings that is less than honest, open, and caring has its roots in fear.

*M*en generally have a greater fear of being smothered, while women tend to have a greater fear of abandonment.

The more damaged a woman is, the more she sees the man in her family as her supply of strength. The more damaged a man is, the more he sees the woman and family as threatening his independence.

*B*ecause they share a common emotional background, men who love too little and women who love too much tend to team up with each other. This, of course, compounds the problems they each unconsciously brought to the relationship.

When we have been damaged and are not healed, we tend to be dangerous.

*R*elationship-handicapped men and women raise relationship-handicapped sons and
daughters.

July 19

*T*he word "love" is constantly applied to various states of arousal that actually embody what love is *not*.

Lust, passion, jealously, suffering, fear, excitement, greed, seduction, subjugation, relief from boredom or loneliness, vindication, competition, pride, and self-will all commonly masquerade as love.

$\mathcal{P}$ersonal love is not compulsive, it is poised.

*T*he ability to love another person arises from a full heart, not an empty one.

July 22

We make a virtual religion of relationship, laying at its feet the greatest burdens of being human.

We have no business asking of another human being what we should be asking of God.

Who is good for us? The person who does not diminish our contact with our Higher Power.

$\mathcal{A}$s long as spiritual contact is our *first* priority, relationship issues will sort themselves out.

*R*eliance on something larger than ourselves and other than the relationship must be present in order to love freely, deeply, and well.

July 26

$\mathcal{W}$ithout reliance on a Higher Power, fear of loss of a relationship grows where love should.

*W*ithout mutual trust and respect, many of those stirrings that are called love but are really obsession can take root and grow—but love cannot.

Jealousy   Dependency Insecurity

*W*ith codependency, everyone is waiting for the addict to recover (which may never happen) before they can be happy.

When you learn to be happy no matter what someone else is doing, you are recovering—and you increase others' chances of recovering, too.

*T*he most help is to be had from the most focused approach, so it is important to find a program attended by others who share our condition.

With a program for recovery, we no longer have to relive our childhoods in our adult relationships.

$\mathcal{L}$ike no one else, people who share our path of recovery can appreciate and applaud our progress.

*E*very day, look at yourself in the mirror, say your name, and then say, "I love you and accept you exactly the way you are."

$\mathcal{Y}$ou are a necessary and beloved part of the universe. You don't have to earn your right to exist.

When a *man* is a relationship addict, we can see the disease for what it really is, free of the cultural stereotypes that reinforce loving too much in women.

*E*very woman in this culture is actively encouraged by magazines and other media to behave in most of the ways that are typical of a very sick relationship addict.

Our culture actually encourages relationship addiction among women and has sanctions against women who do not think, feel, and act in these ways.

*W*hile it is true that relationship-addicted women tend to find "nice" men boring, there is another factor to be considered. Finding a nice man and learning to love him isn't an automatic solution to our problems, because, for one thing, not all nice men are really nice. Some simply have developed a very quiet and covert way of operating dishonestly in relationships.

*G*iving and giving to another person really amounts to unacknowledged bribery.

Why are we resented instead of appreciated for all we've done? The answer is: Because we haven't been honest; we've been manipulative.

The incredible irony of relationship addiction is that at the core of the obsession lies deep fear of intimacy.

$\mathcal{I}$n many partnerships it is difficult to tell who is the more dependent and needy, no matter which partner *appears* to be the relationship addict.

*N*o one, ever, should be looking for a therapist for another person.

When we try to get another person into therapy, our motive is self-interest operating under the guise of being helpful.

$\mathcal{L}$ooking frantically for answers is not the route to recovery. When we become totally willing to recover, *no matter what,* the route to recovery reveals itself.

$\mathcal{S}$haring our experiences, good or bad, in a program of recovery is a part of recovery itself.

$\mathcal{R}$ecovery, in men and women, occurs when it is pursued for its own sake, rather than for the effect it will have on the partnership or marriage.

When people truly are working on their own recoveries, they don't flaunt whatever they're doing to impress others with their sincerity. If you're tempted to prove to him how much you've changed, you need to make sure your "recovery" is not just another move in the deadly dance performed by two partners locked in the strangling embrace of obstinacy.

$\mathcal{I}$f, from childhood on, you've had to take care of and understand everyone else, you probably never learned to take care of and understand yourself.

*I*f you came from a chaotic background, as an adult you'll find the greater the difficulties of an encounter, the more exciting and arousing it is.

$\mathcal{A}$s long as our attention is on the state of our relationship with another person at the expense of developing a relationship with our own inner self, the capacity for intimacy will not increase.

*W*e must accept and love our own inner being before we can tolerate another person coming close enough to know and love us.

$\mathcal{W}$e don't get stepped on if we aren't already lying down.

$\mathcal{S}$hould one person shift position, the entire structure of the relationship or family is automatically changed. Therefore we change our situation most by changing ourselves.

*U*nfortunately, many of us prefer the stagnant status quo to the challenge of making changes that would improve the quality of our lives.

$\mathcal{Y}$ou must acknowledge the possibility that when you stop loving too much, your relationship may end.

$\mathcal{S}$ometimes the emptiness will be so deep you will almost be able to feel the wind blowing through the place where your heart should be. Embrace the emptiness and know that you will not always feel this way, and that just by holding still and feeling it you will begin to fill up with the warmth of self-acceptance.

$\mathcal{L}$ife improves in direct relation to the degree that we become more true to ourselves.

*I*n recovery, retaining our poise becomes a higher priority than either arousing pity or taking revenge.

$\mathcal{A}$ marriage that was supposed to be the solution to old problems and old pain often becomes the biggest, most painful problem of all.

*I*f you are a battered woman, consider applying the concept of relationship addiction, with its roots in childhood trauma and its drive to right old wrongs, to yourself and your condition. Doing so will allow you to begin your own recovery instead of waiting for him to change.

$\mathcal{I}$t is through the work of forgiveness that we learn the lesson for which our soul has chosen this lifetime.

Our recovery requires a lot of time and work and dedication, but continuing to love too much costs a great deal more.

*I*n a support group of peers where no one is the expert and all are equals, we each become responsible for finding our own truths.

$\mathcal{L}$earning to interact sexually with another person in an intimate, rather than competitive and essentially hostile, way is a tremendous piece of work for many relationship-addicted women.

$\mathcal{R}$elationship addiction is the most romanticized addiction of all.

$\mathcal{S}$exual involvement for those who are achieving recovery from loving too much is based on the tenderness of truly caring about another human being and on the excitement of shared intimacy, rather than on the struggle to make a conquest of an impossible lover.

*W*ithout recovery, when we think the issue is about whether or not we should leave, it is usually really about winning versus losing.

Ironically, it's easier to leave, if that's what we finally need to do, after we have some recovery under our belts, because recovery doesn't mean winning—it means not playing.

$\mathscr{A}$ddiction develops when reliance on the drug, substance, or activity evolves from being a choice to being a compulsion.

*W*e, as a culture, have ways of "dressing up" addictions to make them look like free choices rather than compulsions.

*I*f we took on too much responsibility at too early an age, we may have been pretending to be grown up for so long, asking for so little for ourselves and doing so much for others that by now it seems too late to take our turn.

But it isn't.

Begin to learn how to take your turn now.

$\mathcal{W}$e need to address our struggles for meaning, for identity, and for understanding within a spiritual quest, not a relationship quest.

$\mathcal{M}$ost of us who love too much have already learned the great spiritual lesson of compassion. In fact, many of us *overdo* compassion. We want to do for others what they really should be doing for themselves.

We are now ready for the next great spiritual lesson—detachment. We must learn to detach—with love and compassion—from those whose lives we are trying to control.

*T*he need to control others under the guise of being helpful is very typical of the relationship addict.

When we love too much, healing ourselves means that we must *stop* looking for ways to help others.

$\mathcal{W}$hen we let go of performing in certain ways in order to gain others' approval and love, we begin to learn who we really are.

When we become willing to forgive another person, suddenly we are given all the understanding we need of that person's condition.

*S*pirituality, like charity, begins at home. We might think that with fewer problems and more time to ponder deep truths, we could better develop our spiritual side. But it is precisely through dealing with life's problems and pressures that our character defects are exposed and eventually, through much effort, refined.

We finally become more tolerant, compassionate, understanding, able to detach with love, etc., and less self-willed, fearful, interfering, and controlling because we *must* in order to survive with some degree of serenity in the emotional arena of life.

This is spiritual development.

*A*s we become more able to accept people *as they are,* we become more able to choose those who are good for us and to bless and release those who are not.

*T*he first time we find ourselves on our knees, we're usually desperate for help.

Later, humbly praying becomes a valued part of our efforts to receive guidance in order to live as we're meant to.

Finally, because we recognize the invaluable function prayer has served in our spiritual awakening, we're able to give thanks for the very problems that brought us to our knees in the first place.

*I*n order to recover you may have to let go of the mistaken idea that your high degree of sexual attraction or lust has, or ever did have, anything to do with love.

September 15

When we've made significant progress in a given area, life sometimes provides us with a test that shows whether or not we've really learned our lesson—kind of like a final exam that we must pass at the end of a school term so that we can go on to the next level of our education.

For instance, just when you have finally gotten over a man, he may call—and you may be tempted to see him to prove to him and to yourself that the relationship really is finished. This is a dangerous move. In order to pass this test, you are not required to see him and survive with your heart intact. You are required to forego seeing him at all.

*I*f we want to change our lives, it is more important that we change our attitudes rather than our circumstances. Unless we change our attitudes, it is unlikely that our circumstances will ever really change.

$\mathcal{E}$xcept for the physical abuse and/or emotional humiliation, the violent relationship, with all its intensity, best fits our culture's idea of how "real love" is expressed.

No woman in a stable, healthy relationship is ever wooed with the intensity that an abuser directs toward his partner in the courtship and honeymoon phases of the syndrome of violence.

One of the payoffs for the abused woman is that during the honeymoon phase, after the battering, she feels strong and powerful and in control of her partner.

The need to control the batterer is usually the victim's strongest motive for being in the relationship.

If you are a battered woman, you are a relationship addict with a life-threatening disease for which there is a program of recovery.

*I*t's vital that we see our failures as lessons—and more than that, as our pathway to God. After all, it isn't what we do well that brings about our spiritual surrender, but what we cannot do at all.

September 19

$\mathcal{R}$ecovery from loving too much is for those who *want* it, not for those who *need* it. Most women *need* to recover from all the big and little ways they harm themselves and others through forcing issues, trying to manage and control people and events, practicing denial, and indulging their self-will. But few of us *want* to work on ourselves more than we want to work on someone else. So we keep on trying to change what we can't instead of what we can.

$\mathcal{E}$very problem is a pathway to God, designed by your soul to get your attention.

*W*hen our recovery becomes our *first* priority, when our attention is on it rather than him, then our higher self steps in and does for us what we cannot do on our own.

September 22

When something or someone isn't the way we'd like, we can either stay poised or indulge in an emotional binge.

Staying poised lets us hang on to our dignity, build up our self-esteem, and deepen our serenity.

Indulging in nagging, scolding, crying, pleading, raging, and threatening, like any other binge, leaves us with a hangover.

$\mathcal{H}$ealing comes through a change of consciousness, a change of heart.

Healing comes through forgiveness of ourselves, forgiveness of life and of God.

Healing comes when we relinquish our beliefs about what *should* be and become willing to accept and eventually even appreciate what simply *is.*

*E*very illness, every injury, every experience of suffering serves ultimately to cleanse and to purify.

Though we may not always understand exactly how this takes place, if we keep this teaching in mind, then we may begin to discern some of the valuable ways our difficulties serve us.

*P*hysical illness can serve as an indicator of our psychological evasions. It alerts us that an issue demands to be addressed, and makes ignoring that issue sufficiently painful to get our attention.

Through the very symptoms it manifests, the body can point to whatever we're trying to deny.

*T*he design of your life cannot be readily seen while you're busy living it.

Trust not only that there *is* a design and that it's beautiful, but that the more you trust it, the more beautiful it becomes.

*E*very difficult situation in life is a test, and as we evolve, so do our tests, from situations that try our physical courage to those that try our moral courage, our personal integrity, and our capacity for self-knowledge.

None of these tests is easy, but once we've passed a test, we don't have to repeat it *at the same level* ever again.

When it looks as though the same test has reappeared again, either we haven't yet learned its lesson or we're learning it on a deeper, more profound level.

September 28

*R*emember that we get worse until we get better, that we go deeper into the problem *in order* to finally surrender to healing it—whatever that might mean.

*E*very situational challenge is a spiritual challenge as well. The greater the challenge, the greater the *potential* for spiritual growth.

*O*ur souls don't give us choices about the patterns of our lives. They know what we need to experience, and they cause us to attract those needed experiences without our conscious consent.

But we *do* have choices as to how we confront those experiences. This is where our free will operates.

*W*ill you, like an alchemist striving to extract gold from base metals, search for what is precious among the dreariest and most discouraging aspects of your life?

If you do, you *will* find it there, awaiting your conscious discovery.

*M*any, many women who love too much discover that this obsession with another person represents, on a daily basis, ninety percent or more of who they are in terms of their thoughts, feelings, behavior, and use of their personal energy. Only ten percent is left over for dealing with *every other* aspect of life.

We may, in the depths of difficulty and despair, long for a happier history and more promising present conditions.

For our spiritual development, however, our antagonists and afflictions are necessary foils against which we test ourselves in order to grow into all we are ultimately capable of being.

October 4

$\mathcal{S}$ome parents provide the welcome gifts of love, security, understanding, and support, while other parents offer far less welcome and comforting qualities and conditions. Yet these, too, are gifts.

Perhaps, in your family of origin . . .

a cold, indifferent mother forced you to abandon your clinging dependence and stand on your own two feet, or . . .

a critical and disapproving father caused you, in striving for his approval, to take on challenges you wouldn't otherwise have attempted, until one day you realized what incredible things you've accomplished, or . . .

a subtly cruel mother or father sensitized you to how easily a word, look, or gesture could wound, and now you are more consciously compassionate in your daily life than you otherwise would have been.

While you may wish yours had been a more ideal childhood, you need to acknowledge that less-than-perfect parents and conditions quite possibly provided the necessary pressure for whatever maturity, growth, and understanding you can claim today.

*D*eveloping your spirituality requires *willingness,* not faith.

Often with willingness comes faith.

If you don't want faith, you probably won't get it, but with a spiritual practice you will still find more serenity than you've had before.

October 6

Whether or not you believe in God, and, if you do, whether or not you're on speaking terms with Him, you can still develop your spirituality.

Find out what brings you peace and serenity, and commit some time, at least half an hour
daily, to that practice. This discipline can and
will bring you relief and comfort.

*I*f you want to get over a heartbreaking end to a relationship with as much speed and as little pain as possible, do this:

Every time he comes into your thoughts, pray as sincerely as you can for his highest good.

Period.

Do not try to define what his highest good *is*, e.g., that he grows up or appreciates how good you were for him, or quits drinking or leaves his new girlfriend and comes back to you. You cannot know what his highest good is—only God knows that.

Even if it's taken you years to get over relationships before, you'll be amazed at how quickly you'll heal when you take this approach.

When we measure the degree of our love by the depth of our torment, we are loving too much.

The bad news is: There are no shortcuts out of the pattern of loving too much.

Should you decide that you really do want to change, it will require—as all therapeutic change does—years of work and nothing short of your total commitment.

The good new is: If you choose to begin the process of recovery, you *will* change from a woman who loves someone else so much it hurts into a woman who loves herself enough to stop the pain.

*W*hen you want to pick up the phone to call that impossible man, you are facing the same struggle as an alcoholic wanting to pick up that drink.

*W*ithin each person is an incredibly strong need to wrest a happy ending from even the most disastrous emotional alliances. This need in a woman who loves too much can be dangerous, even life-threatening.

As women who love too much, we like to believe that we are capable of deep intimacy even though our partners aren't. However, we all tend to choose as partners people who are capable of the same level of intimacy as we are.

If our partners cannot tolerate intimacy, we're with them probably because we can't either. Because closeness actually feels threatening, it's easier for us to keep wishing for it than to actually live with it.

Ironically, when we stop defining a partner as "the problem," a greater degree of intimacy gradually becomes possible between us.

Our work is ever with ourselves, with changing our own hearts.

*W*hen you read a self-help book and underline all the passages you think would help *him*, you are loving too much.

*S*ometimes, even long after we're parted from someone, we are driven to find out about him—what he's doing, whom (if anyone) he's seeing, etc.

It is a spiritual law that what we are meant to know will be revealed to us *without any effort on our part.* We are wise to trust the soul's timing as well as its methods regarding such disclosures.

Anything else amounts to forcing issues, which is part of our disease.

*I*t is the acceptance of another *as he is* that allows him to change *if he chooses to do so.*

$\mathcal{M}$ost of us have the ability to be far happier and more fulfilled as individuals than we realize. Often, we don't claim that happiness because we believe someone *else's* behavior is preventing us from doing so. We ignore our obligation to develop ourselves while we scheme and maneuver and manipulate to change someone else, and we become angry and discouraged and depressed when our efforts fail. Trying to change someone else is frustrating and depressing, but exercising the power we have to effect change in our own lives is exhilarating.

A woman who uses her relationships as a drug will have fully as much denial about that fact as any chemically addictive individual, and fully as much resistance and fear concerning letting go of her obsessive thinking and highly emotionally charged way of interacting with men.

*F*or the woman who loves too much, her primary disease is her addiction to the pain and familiarity of an unrewarding relationship. True, this generates from lifelong patterns reaching back into childhood, but she *must* first of all deal with her patterns in the present in order for her recovery to begin. No matter how sick or cruel or helpless her partner is, she must understand that her every attempt to change him, help him, control him, or blame him is a manifestation of her disease, and that she must stop these behaviors before other areas of her life improve. Her only legitimate work is with herself.

*Y*ou may find there is very little to talk about once all the cajoling, arguing, threatening, fighting, and making up comes to an end. That's because all this time you've had a relationship with the man you thought he could, should, and would be—with your help—instead of with the man he really is.

October 21

*O*ne of the implications of letting go of managing and controlling others is that you must relinquish the identity of "being helpful," but ironically, that very act of letting go is frequently the single most helpful thing you can do for the one you love. The identity of "being helpful" is an ego trip. If you really want to be helpful, let go of his problems and help yourself.

*I*f you find yourself participating in a no-win cycle of accusation, rebuttal, blame, and counterblame, stop. Let go of trying to make it turn out the way you want it to by being nice, being angry, or being helpless. Stop needing to win. Stop even needing to fight or to make him give you a good reason or excuse for his behavior or neglect. Stop needing him to be sufficiently sorry.

*M*ost of us who love too much are caught up in blaming others for the unhappiness in our lives, while denying our own faults and our own choices. This is an insidiously seductive approach to life that must be rooted out and eliminated, and the way to do so is to take a good, hard, honest look at ourselves. Only by seeing our problems and our faults (and our good points and successes) as *ours,* rather than related somehow to others, can we take the steps to change what needs to be changed.

$\mathcal{B}$e willing to try at least one brand-new activity each week. Look at life as a smorgasbord, and help yourself to lots of different experiences so that you can discover what appeals to you.

*C*ultivating whatever needs to be developed in yourself means not waiting for him to change before you get on with life. Instead of making your plans dependent on his cooperation, make them as though you had no one but yourself on whom to lean. Consider how you would do it if you didn't even know him. You'll find there are many exciting ways to make life work for you when you stop depending on him and instead make use of all your other options.

$\mathscr{W}$hen you don't like many of his basic characteristics, values, and behaviors, but you put up with them thinking that if you are only attractive and loving enough he'll want to change for you, you are loving too much.

*A*ny significant relationship actually has an independent life of its own, with a purpose quite hidden from our conscious awareness. Indeed, all relationships exist for a very different reason than we believe either individually or collectively as a society. Their true purpose is *not* to make us happy, *not* to meet our needs, *not* to define us or our niche in society, *not* to keep us safe . . . but to cause us to wake up and grow up.

Waking up is uncomfortable, and growing up is hard. No wonder something as compelling as a relationship is often required to get the job done.

*W*hen our relationships jeopardize our emotional well-being and perhaps even our physical health and safety, we are definitely loving too much.

*I*f you have ever found yourself obsessed with a man, you may have suspected that the root of that obsession was not love but fear. We who love obsessively are full of fear—fear of being alone, fear of being unlovable and unworthy, fear of being ignored or abandoned or destroyed. We give our love in the desperate hope that the man with whom we're obsessed will take care of our fears. Instead, the fears—and our obsessions—deepen until giving love in order to get it back becomes a driving force in our lives. And because our strategy doesn't work, we try, we love, even harder. We love too much.

*R*ecovery is not a door to be closed on an old way of living, but one that must be opened daily to a fuller experience of being alive.

$\mathcal{S}$ome men are as relationship addicted as any woman could be, and their feelings and behaviors issue from the same kinds of childhood experiences and dynamics. However, most men who have been damaged in childhood try to protect themselves and avoid their pain through pursuits that are more external than internal, more impersonal than personal. Men tend to direct their obsession toward work, sports, or hobbies, whereas women do not. Instead, women tend to focus their obsession intensely on a relationship—perhaps with just such a damaged and distant man.

*W*e all tend to deny what is too painful or too threatening for us to accept.

November 2

*I*t is one of the ironies of life that we women can respond with such sympathy and understanding to the pain in one another's lives while remaining so blinded to (and by) the pain in our own.

*R*edirect your loving attention away from your obsession with a man and toward your own recovery and your own life.

*L*oving too much is a pattern learned early and practiced well, and to give it up will be frightening, threatening, and constantly challenging.

*O*ur physical bodies *cannot lie.* Therefore, they are important indicators of what we're *really* feeling. However, for some of us, being uncomfortable has been our accustomed state for so long that we don't even know, until we have some recovery under out belts, what it is to live without knots in our stomachs.

Once we have some recovery and can feel the difference, we are less likely to do things and live in ways that cause the knots to come back.

$\mathcal{L}$oving too much does not mean loving too many men or falling in love too often or having too great a depth of genuine love for another. It means, in truth, obsessing about a man and calling that obsession love.

Brad, Brad, Brad, Brad, Brad, Brad, Brad Brad...

What all unhealthy relationships have in common is the partners' inability to discuss *root* problems. There may be other problems that *are* discussed, often ad nauseum, but these often cover up the underlying secrets that make the relationship dysfunctional. It is the degree of secrecy—the inability to talk about these root problems—rather than their severity that defines both how dysfunctional a relationship becomes and how severely its members are damaged.

*T*hat the men who attract us most strongly are those who appear to be needy makes sense if we understand that it is our own wish to be loved and helped that is at the root of the attraction.

*I*f any of your efforts on his behalf include:

- buying him clothes to improve his self-image;

- finding a therapist for him and begging him to go;

- financing expensive hobbies to help him use his time better;

- going through disruptive geographic relocations because "he's not happy here";

- giving him half or all of your property and possessions so he won't feel inferior to you;

- providing him with a place to live so that he can feel secure;

- allowing him to abuse you emotionally because "he was never allowed to express his feelings before"; or

- finding him a job,

you are *definitely* loving too much.

*I*f we had relationships with men who were everything we wanted, what would they need us for? All that talent (and compulsion) for helping would have nowhere to operate. A major part of our identity would be out of a job. So we choose men who are not what we want—and we dream on.

*T*ruly unhealthy relationships simply serve the same function for us as very strong drugs. Their dramatic ups and downs create equally powerful distractions from our own lives and feelings. Without such men on whom to focus, we go into withdrawal, often with many of the same physical and emotional symptoms that accompany actual drug withdrawal: nausea, sweating, chills, shaking, pacing, obsessive thinking, depression, inability to sleep, panic, and anxiety attacks. In an effort to relieve these symptoms, we return to our previous partners or desperately seek new ones.

*A*ll women who love too much carry the emotional backlog of experiences that could lead them to abuse mind-altering substances in order to escape their feelings. But children of chemically dependent parents also tend to inherit a genetic predisposition to substance abuse.

Any chemical addiction must be addressed *first,* before addressing relationship addiction, because the use of mind-altering substances makes refraining from practicing other addictive behaviors, including all our favorite varieties of loving too much, impossible.

When you excuse his moodiness, bad temper, indifference, and put-downs as problems caused by an unhappy childhood, and you try to become his therapist, you are loving too much.

$\mathcal{W}$e find the unstable man exciting, the unreliable man challenging, the unpredictable man romantic, the immature man charming, the moody man mysterious. The angry man needs our understanding. The unhappy man needs our comforting. The inadequate man needs our encouragement, and the cold man needs our warmth. But we cannot "fix" a man who is fine just as he is.

We all have strong emotional reactions to words like *alcoholism, incest, violence,* and *addiction,* and sometimes we cannot look at our own lives realistically because we are so afraid of having these labels apply to us or to those we love. Sadly, our inability to use the words when they do apply often precludes our getting appropriate help.

*S*elf-will means believing that you alone have all the answers. Letting go of self-will means becoming willing to hold still, be open, and wait for guidance for yourself.

When we love too much, every sexual encounter carries all our striving to change this man. With every kiss and every touch we work at communicating to him how special and worthy he is, how much he is admired and cherished. We feel sure that once he is convinced of our love, he will be metamorphosed into his true self, awakened to the embodiment of everything we want and need him to be.

At the bottom of all our efforts to change someone else is a basically selfish motive, a belief that through his changing we will become happy. There is nothing wrong with wanting to be happy, but to place the source of that happiness outside ourselves, in someone else's hands, means we are denying our abilities to change our own lives for the better, and refusing to take responsibility for doing so.

*W*hat we manifest in our lives is a reflection of what is deep inside us: our beliefs about our own worth, our right to happiness, what we deserve in life. When those beliefs change, so do our lives.

*R*ecognize what reality is and allow that reality to be, without needing to change it. Therein lies a happiness that issues not from manipulating outside conditions or people, but from developing inner peace, even in the face of challenges and difficulties.

$\mathcal{T}$here are *no* mistakes in life, only lessons, so get out there and let yourself learn some of what life wants to teach you.

When you let go of blaming others and take responsibility for your own choices, you become free to embrace all kinds of options that were not available to you when you saw yourself as a victim of others. This prepares you to begin to change those things in your life that are either not good for you or are no longer satisfying or fulfilling—to let go of what you've outgrown and embark on fresh paths and projects.

*I*t is common for people with addictions to team up with others like themselves. Then each person tries to control the other's problem.

$\mathcal{D}$o two things each day that you don't want to do, in order to stretch yourself and expand your idea of who you are and what you are capable of doing.

*B*oth alcoholism and loving too much are subtle diseases in their early stages. By the time it is obvious that something very destructive is in progress, the temptation is to look at and treat the physical manifestations—the alcoholic's liver or pancreas, the relationship-addicted woman's nerves or high blood pressure—without accurately assessing the entire picture. It is vital to view these "symptoms" in the overall context of the diseases that have created them, and to recognize the existence of these diseases at the earliest possible time in order to halt the continued destruction of emotional and physical health.

$\mathcal{L}$earn to give to yourself. Give time, give attention. We need to learn that we ourselves can be the source of good things in our lives.

*I*f you balk at spending time and money on your own recovery because it seems wasteful, consider how much time and money you have spent trying to avoid the pain from either being in an unhappy relationship or from having it end. Drinking, using drugs, eating too much, taking trips to get away from it all, having to replace things (either his or yours) that were broken in fits of anger, missing work, expensive long-distance phone calls to him or to someone you hope will understand, buying him presents to make up, buying yourself presents to help you forget, spending days and nights crying over him, neglecting your health to the point where you become seriously ill— the list of ways you have spent time and money because of loving too much is probably long enough to make you very uncomfortable if you look at it honestly. Recovery requires that you be willing to invest at least that much in getting well. And as an investment, it is guaranteed to give you gratifying dividends.

We achieve a sense of self from what we do for ourselves and how we develop our own capacities. If all your efforts have gone into helping others develop, you're bound to feel empty. Start to nurture and develop your own capacities now.

November 29

*D*eveloping your spirituality basically means *letting go of self-will,* of the determination to make things happen the way you think they should. Instead, you must accept the fact that you may not know what is best in a given situation either for yourself or for another person.

A carefree, irresponsible man makes a charming acquaintance but is a poor prospect for a satisfying relationship. Until you can give yourself permission to be more free and easy, you'll need him to create the fun and excitement in your life.

$\mathcal{B}$y developing your spirituality you have tools for finding relief that don't require that you manipulate anyone else into doing or being what you want. No one has to change in order for you to feel good. Because you have access to spiritual nourishment, your life and your happiness come to be more under your own control and less vulnerable to the actions of others.

The less you need a partner, the better partner you become—and the healthier partner
you will attract (and be attracted to).

*T*he changes you are making in your life require that those around you change, too, and they will naturally resist. But unless you give credence to their indignation, it will be fairly short-lived. It is just an attempt to push you back into your old, selfless behavior, into doing for them what they can and should do for themselves.

*Y*ou must listen carefully to your inner voice regarding what is good for you, right for you, and then follow it. This is how you develop healthy self-interest, by listening to your own cues. Up to now you've probably been nearly psychic at picking up other people's cues about how they wanted you to behave. Tune those cues out, or they'll continue to drown out your own.

$\mathcal{D}$etaching, which is vital to your recovery, requires that you disentangle your ego from his feelings and especially from his actions and their results. It requires that you allow him to deal with the consequences of his behavior, that you don't save him from *any* of his pain. You may continue to care *about* him, but you don't take care *of* him. You allow him to find his own way, just as you are working to find yours.

$\mathcal{R}$ecognize that your worth is great, that your talents are worthy of expression, that your fulfillment is as important as anyone else's, and that your best self is the greatest gift you have to give the world as a whole and, most especially, those closest to you.

*W*hen you are really ready to stop managing or controlling the man in your life, this also means that you must stop encouraging and praising him. Why? Because chances are you have used praise and encouragement to try to get him to do what you'd like, and therefore they must be numbered among your tools for manipulating him. Praising and encouraging are very close to pushing, and when you do that you are trying again to take control of his life. Think about why you are lauding something he's done. Is it to help raise his self-esteem? That's manipulation. Is it so he will continue whatever behavior you're praising? That's manipulation. Is it so that he'll know how proud you are of him? That can be a burden for him to carry. Let him develop his own pride from his own accomplishments. Otherwise, you come dangerously close to playing a mothering role with him. He doesn't need another mother (no matter how bad his mother was!), and much more to the point, you don't need him to be your child.

As you become better able to nurture yourself, you may find that you've attracted someone who is able to nurture you. As we become healthier and more balanced, we attract healthier and more balanced partners. As we become less needy, more of our needs are met. As we give up the role of supernurturer, we make space for someone to nurture us.

*T*here are several phases in recovering from loving too much. The first phase begins when we realize what we are doing and wish we could stop. Next comes our willingness to get help for ourselves, followed by our actual initial attempt to secure help. After that, we enter the phase of recovery that requires our commitment to our own healing and our willingness to continue with our recovery program. During this period we begin to change how we act, think, and feel. What once felt normal and familiar begins to feel uncomfortable and unhealthy. We enter the next phase of recovery when we start making choices that no longer follow our old patterns but enhance our lives and promote our well-being instead. Throughout the stages of recovery, self-love grows slowly and steadily. First we stop hating ourselves, then we become more tolerant ofr ourselves. Next, there is a burgeoning appreciation of our good qualities, and then self-acceptance develops. Finally, genuine self-love evolves.

*I*t isn't possible to be too intelligent or too attractive or too charming or too well-bred or too well-off or too well-educated or too talented or too successful to love too much.

None of these conditions prevents or precludes relationship addiction or, for that matter, any other kind of addiction.

As we recover from loving too much, we change how we relate to our parents and to our children. With our parents we become less needy and less angry, and often less ingratiating as well. We become much more honest, often more tolerant, and sometimes more genuinely loving. With our children we become less controlling, less worried, and less guilty. We relax and enjoy our children more because we are able to relax and enjoy ourselves more. As we feel greater freedom to pursue our own needs and interests, they are freed to do the same.

When we are no longer loving too much, friends with whom we could once commiserate endlessly may now strike us as obsessed and unhealthy. Mutual misery as a criterion for friendship is replaced by more rewarding mutual interests. So what frequently happens with recovery is that as our patterns of relating change, so do our circles of friends.

December 13

*N*o matter how open, accepting, and genuinely loving we become with recovery, there will still be people whose anger, hostility, and aggression will inhibit us from being all these things in their presence. To be vulnerable with them is to be masochistic. Therefore, lowering our boundaries and eventually eliminating them should happen only with people—friends, relatives, or lovers—with whom we have a relationship bathed in trust, love, respect, and reverence for our shared, tender humanity.

*I*f what we have been doing all along really worked, we wouldn't need to recover.

We have nothing to lose by beginning to recover. We're already enduring alarming levels of pain with no prospect of relief unless we change. What holds us back is fear, fear of the unknown.

Don't let that fear of relinquishing what you've always known and done and been hold you back from your metamorphosis into a healthier, higher, more truly loving self.

*R*ecovery begins when we become willing to channel the energy and effort formerly spent on practicing our disease into pursuing our recovery instead.

*I*f we love too much, men who appeal to us usually have problems. They need not necessarily be penniless or in ill health, however. Perhaps they are unable to relate well to others, or are cold and unaffectionate, or stubborn or selfish, or sulking or melancholy. Maybe they are a bit wild and irresponsible, or unable to make commitments or be faithful. Or maybe they tell us they have never been able to love anyone. Depending on our own backgrounds, we will respond to different varieties of neediness. But respond we will, with the conviction that these men need our help, our compassion, and our wisdom in order to improve their lives.

When most of our conversations with intimate friends are about him, his problems, his thoughts, his feelings, and nearly all our sentences begin with "he . . ." we are loving too much.

$\mathcal{I}$f something isn't good for us, it isn't really good for anyone else either.

When we are lonely and lost, we don't simply yearn for company, but for our own kind. The most powerful and profound sources of healing available are groups made up of people dedicated to speaking honestly with one another about a common problem, and self-led according to simple guidelines and spiritual principles.

*I*t is a very high form of love to allow someone for whom we care deeply to suffer the natural consequences of his or her behavior and to learn thereby.

$\mathcal{U}$nderstand that with relationship addiction, slips are inevitable and at first discouragingly frequent. Every day we don't practice relationship addiction is both a priceless gift and a splendid achievement.

*O*nce our self-acceptance and self-love begin to develop and take hold, we are then ready to consciously practice simply being ourselves without trying to please, without performing in certain ways calculated to gain another's approval and love. But awkwardness and a feeling of great vulnerability come over us when we are just *being* rather than *doing,* and to stop performing feels at first like being frozen. Finally, in time, our *genuine* loving impulses have a chance to be heard and felt and to assert themselves.

*T*o fully begin recovery, first learn how to *hold* still.

Then learn how to *be* still.

When you can hear and feel and know *stillness,* you can hear and feel and know God.

*H*umor is one of the great hallmarks of recovery. When we find amusing some of the same aspects of our lives that used to bring on tears, rage, or despair, we are definitely well on our way to a healthier approach to living.

It is probably true for us that genuine recovery requires humor, and that genuine humor requires recovery.

Taking responsibility for yourself and your happiness gives great freedom to children who have felt guilty and responsible for your unhappiness (which they always do). A child can never hope to balance the scales or repay the debt when a parent has sacrificed her life, her happiness, her fulfillment for the child or the family. Seeing a parent fully embrace life gives the child permission to do the same, just as seeing a parent suffer indicates to the child that suffering is what life is all about.

*R*ecovery requires that you change—but trying too hard to change too much too quickly will very likely ensure that you never really change at all.

When you pray for help to change, pray as well to be able to wait patiently while the changes are taking place.

$\mathcal{L}$ife's unfolding events may be welcome or unwelcome, but whether they are fortunate or unfortunate can be discerned only in the fullness of time.

*A*lthough every woman reading this book may have in common the tendency to love too much, nevertheless each of us has her own particular pattern for doing so.

For clues to your personal style, consider the common themes expressed in your favorite work of fiction, your favorite film, your favorite song, poem, fairy tale, etc. Taken together they will almost certainly provide you with insight into how you go about the business of living and loving—too much.

$\mathscr{I}$f you are truly on the path of recovery from loving too much, know that you are a miracle.

Notes